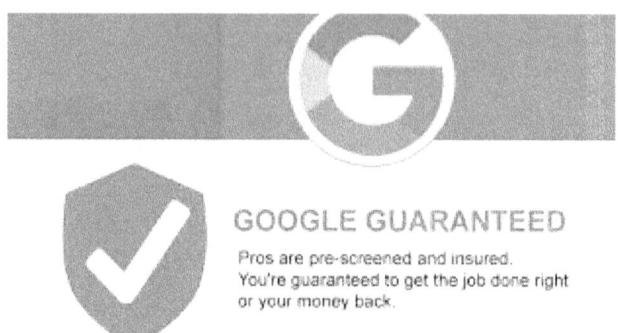

# THE COMPLETE

# GUIDE

## Google Local Ads

### 2021

### Google Guarantee Badge

### "A Quick Guide for Service Oriented Businesses Looking to Increase Revenue"

*Written and Published by Jeremy D. Goding*

### Text Copyright © Jeremy D. Goding

All rights reserved. No part of this guide may be reproduced in any form without permission in writing from the publisher except in the case of brief quotations embodied in critical articles or reviews.

### Legal & Disclaimer

The information contained in this book and its contents is not designed to replace or take the place of any form of medical or professional advice; and is not meant to replace the need for independent medical, financial, legal or other professional advice or services, as may be required. The content and information in this book have been provided for educational and entertainment purposes only.

The content and information contained in this book has been compiled from sources deemed reliable, and it is accurate to the best of the Author's knowledge, information and belief. However, the Author cannot guarantee its accuracy and validity and cannot be held liable for any errors and/or omissions. Further, changes are periodically made to this book as and when needed. Where appropriate and/or necessary, you must consult a professional (including but not limited to your doctor, attorney, financial advisor or such other professional advisor) before using any of the suggested remedies, techniques, or information in this book.

Upon using the contents and information contained in this book, you agree to hold harmless the Author from and against any damages, costs, and expenses, including any legal fees potentially resulting from the application of any of the information provided by this book. This disclaimer applies to any loss, damages or injury caused by the use and application, whether directly or indirectly, of any advice or information presented, whether for breach of contract, tort, negligence, personal injury, criminal intent, or under any other cause of action.

You agree to accept all risks of using the information presented inside this book.

You agree that by continuing to read this book, where appropriate and/or necessary, you shall consult a professional (including but not limited to your doctor, attorney, or financial advisor or such other advisor as needed) before using any of the suggested remedies, techniques, or information in this book.

Table of Contents

***Introduction***
................................................................................................
...... 5

## Chapter 1: What is Google Guarantee? ........ 7

### What It Covers (In Their Terms) ........ 8

### How I Know This Works ........ 8

### Why Will Google Guarantee Be The Best Thing For Your Business? ........ 8

### Why It's Better ........ 9

### What Businesses Does Google Guarantee Help? ........ 11

### Who can set this up? ........ 12

## Chapter 2: The Basics ........ 14

### Setting Up Your Profile ........ 14

### Reviews and Keeping them ........ 15

### Secret Tip On How To Get First Place All The Time ........ 16

### Insurance ........ 17

*Chapter 3: About Advanced Verification* .................................................................. *18*

Licensing ............................................................................................ 18

Licensing Checks ..................................................................................... 19

The Checklist Required for My Carpet Cleaning Company .................................................. 19

*Chapter 4: Coverage areas* ...................................................................... *20*

Ads Overview ......................................................................................... 20

How Ads Work .......................................................................................... 20

What's In Your Ad? ..................................................................................... 20

How to Create an Ad ................................................................................... 22

COVID Options ........................................................................................ 22

Chapter 5: Local Service Ads ................................................................................ 23

What Hours Should I Put for My Ad? ................................................................ 24

Scheduling Your Ad
............................................................................................................. 24

What about Messaging Options? ............................................................................................. 24

*Chapter 6: Managing Leads* ................................................................ 25

Lead Credit and How It Is Charged ................................................................ 25

Valid Leads
............................................................................................................. 26

Examples of Invalid Leads
............................................................................................................. 26

Types of Charged Leads That Are Eligible for a Credit ......................................................... 27

How to Track Leads
............................................................................................................. 27

*Chapter 7: Lead Disputes and Using the App* ........................................... 28

How to Dispute Leads
............................................................................................................. 28

Local Services Ad App
............................................................................................................. 29

*Chapter 8: Costs and Payment* ............................................................... *30*

**How Much Will the Service Cost?**
........................................................................... 30

**How You're Charged**
...................................................................................................
**31**

*Chapter 9: Ready to Receive Leads through Local Services Ads?* ................................. *32*

**Contact Local Services Support**
............................................................................. 32

**Free Local Services Listings**
........................................................................................ 33

*Chapter 10: Google Screened*
................................................................................. *34*

**How It Works**
...................................................................................................
.......... 34

**Who Google Screened Covers**
............................................................................. 35

**Reports**
...................................................................................................
.................... 35

**Using the Dashboard**
...................................................................................................
36

*Chapter 11: Local Services Onboarding Terms*
............................................................ *37*

7

Information You Submit ................................................................. 37

Minimum Provider Requirements ................................................................. 38

Indemnification and Limitation of Liability ................................................................. 38

Employment ................................................................................................................ 38

Notice of Changes ................................................................................................................ 38

Dispute Resolution Agreement ................................................................. 38

Miscellaneous ................................................................................................................ *39*

*Chapter 12: FAQs* ................................................................. *40*

*Conclusion* ................................................................................................................ *42*

## Introduction

I have been using Google products to grow my service businesses since 2007. Over the years, it has been an emotional roller coaster with all the different types of products and well over a million dollars of my own money spent on the various businesses I started, operated, and then eventually sold.

None of my businesses needed outside assistance with sales because Google held the role as lead salesperson. Google never suffers from sales burnout, or takes days off, which makes it the perfect partner when you're trying to grow your business. From AdWords, AdWords Express, Google Boost, Smart Ads, and Local Places Ads, the new products came with a huge cost, but the results were always impressive and beneficial.

The money wasted learning a new Google Product, even with an "experienced PPC"

manager, can be quite overwhelming. Quite often, there is a disconnection between someone who is experienced in PPC or SEO and the actual intricacies, words, and terms that should be used in your online advertising platforms. For instance, I hired someone to write a PPC campaign for my carpet cleaning company and soon found myself getting calls for jobs such as pressure wash cleaning, or just cleaning, when in fact I only did carpet cleaning. It is nearly impossible for one person to know all the write keywords, and the disconnect can be both frustrating and expensive.

A pay-per-click, or PPC, person tends to be all about making sure they have great conversions to show you every month before auto-running your credit card, but the reality is that the conversions might be based on keywords, such as "really cheap and affordable movers near me" or "who is the cheapest carpet cleaner". This may show online analytic conversions but mean nothing when it comes down to whether or not that is the type of client you truly want, and if an online conversion is comparable to other forms of customer conversion.

Out of all the products over the years, Google Guarantee from the Google Local Ads Platform is an excellent choice for small businesses. I recently had sold my moving company in a multi-million-dollar deal and was getting into carpet cleaning when I stumbled across the Google Guarantee (Local Services Ad) article on a Google help page.

As I started to research it, I quickly learned that Google was onto something big! I was certainly impressed with the new layout for myself as a business owner, but also for my customers.

After using Guarantee for almost a year, I decided to write this guide with all the basics, including my tips and tricks, and how you can make this platform as good as I did overnight.

So, let us jump on it without further ado. Shortly your phone will be ringing with what I

consider to be the most qualified clients I have ever received in over 20 million dollars'

worth of sales over the last decade.

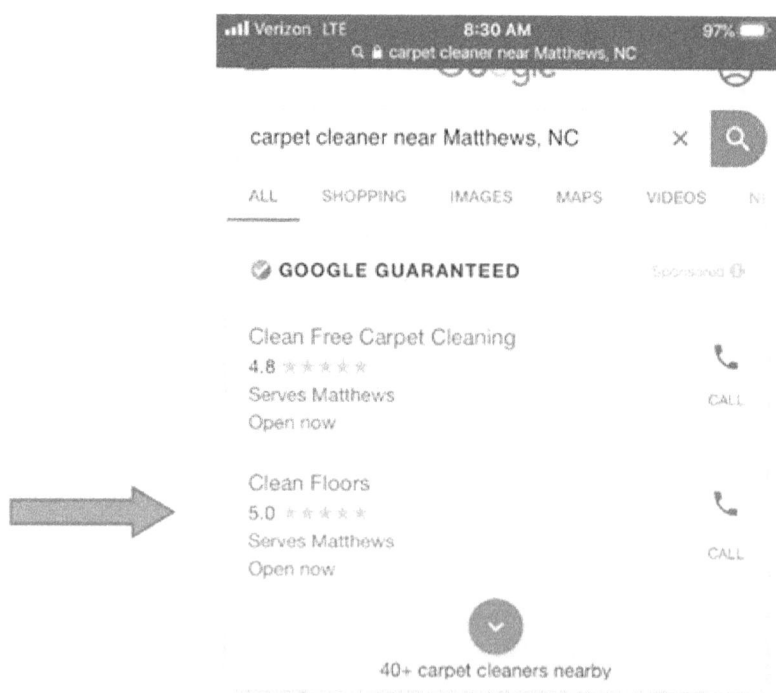

**Chapter 1: What is Google Guarantee?**

Businesses can get a Google Guarantee badge upon passing the Google qualification procedure via its Local Services Platform. (https://ads.google.com/local-services-ads/).

This is a service that charges per lead for calls and messages through the Local Service Platform. Business can also use their Google My Business page (GMB), to get the same verification and pay a fixed monthly charge of $50 to have the Google Guarantee Local Badge show beside their map listing. The cost may vary based on the area. This second option is a great way to show up higher on Google Local Maps and convert more leads since customers are going to feel better about calling you when you are a "verified"

business.

If you are backed by the Google Guarantee, and your customers are not satisfied with the work quality that you provided, Google may refund the amount paid for their service. The upper limits of lifetime coverage for claims are $2,000 in the United States and CAD

$2,000 in Canada. In the 8 months that I've been using Google Guarantee, I have not had a single issue or complaint from my customers. I strongly believe this is because when

people view your business and see your Google Badge that you are verified, they put their trust in you to provide quality service.

### What It Covers (In Their Terms)

This guarantee covers demands amounting to that stated, at the maximum, in the job statement on Google equal to the time cap for reporting. These services must be booked through Google Local Services in order to be covered. The guarantee, however, does not insure add-on or upcoming projects, indemnities to property, discontent with cost, provider reaction, or cancellations.

How it works?

If any of your patrons submit a demand, Google will notify you, so you have a chance to make things right with your customer. If the issue continues and cannot be resolved between you and the customer Google will review the case and resolve the issue.

One important benefit of using Google Guarantee is the lower cost to you as a business owner. Other companies such as HomeAdvisor, and Angel List use the same platform to get you leads and then charge you more than they paid.

### How I Know This Works

If big providers, such as Angel List and HomeAdvisor, are using this platform to resell the leads and increase the lead value by three to four times their amount, then you know it must work for you. Most likely, you will be listed before those outside companies because: 1. I am confident that Local Google Guaranteed Ads come up on serached before national ones from personal experience.

2. Unlike national providers, you will have better reviews overall which will place you higher in the algorithm because you are able to address issues with customers better than local competitors.

### Why Will Google Guarantee Be The Best Thing For Your Business?

Results! That is why Google Guarantee is the best. No, seriously. I have never been happier with any Google Product more than Google Guarantee. The lead to real Customer Conversion has never been better, and the platform seems to funnel in more buyers than

"tire-kickers" or low-price shoppers. I could easily say, without a doubt, that the leads I've

received from using Google Guarantee are higher quality than most leads I've received from other platforms. Another key benefit is that Google Guarantee is a call-only platform which means if the customer wants to reach out they have to do it via phone. This means that when a customer calls, they have done their research and they are often ready to hire.

## Why It's Better

The number one reason why Google Guarantee is better is that you only pay for the calls you accept, or the leads that you respond to off of the platform. Take a minute to think about that. This is an excellent benefit for businesses with low margins because you aren't paying for people who reach out without serious intentions to hire you.

With traditional Google Ads, you pay for the visitors who look at your site, which in most businesses forces you to think about what the customer wants to see when they go on your webpage. If you need a locksmith or carpet cleaner, then what information do you need from a website that you found on google?

With a guaranteed platform, the phone rings, and it is a real customer ready to buy your product. It gives you a chance to sell directly to the customer and have an authentic conversation where you can explain your company, which results in a much higher job booking rate. Finally, it **offers top place positioning above traditional Google Ads and Local Google Map listings**.

Google stays as the king in terms of online search. To be a small local business and have top positioning is an amazing thing which makes a real difference! Google Guarantee gives you that option. Again, in all the years I have been running businesses, I have spent over a million dollars with Google.

Out of all their products, Google Guarantee is by far the best lead service that pulls in customers that are ready to buy right then and there. You will notice a lot less "tire-kicker"

calls that Pay-Per-Click or PPC Campaigns tend to produce.

Ad · www.cleanfloors.com/

Carpet Steam Cleaning @ $45 | 5 Areas Only $99 - Other Deals | cleanfloors.com

7 Days a Week. If You Need a Reliable and Affordable Carpet Steam Cleaner. Carpet Steam Cleaning - Area Rugs - Upholstery Cleaning & More. Service You Trust. Transparent Prices. View Gallery. Schedule A Cleaning. BBB Accredited Business. Get A Free Quote.

📞 Call (704) 669-8703

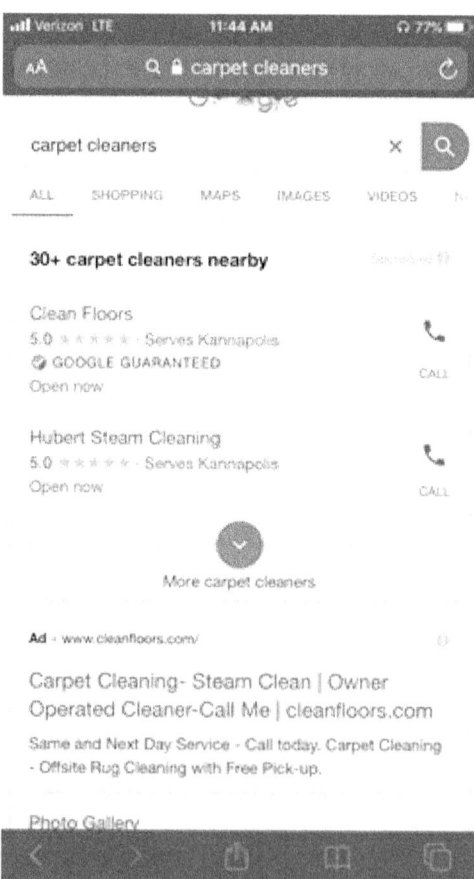

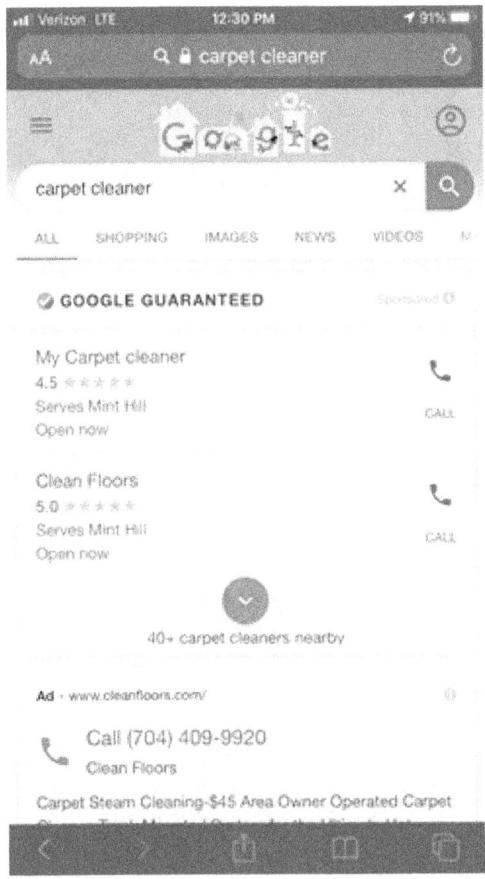

You can also use Guarantee in conjunction with your AdWords Ads to get more bang for your buck. When a customer sees your ad twice in the top three spots, they know this is a company that they can trust, and it surely stands out!

I noticed a decline in clicks to my Adword Accounts when I launched Guarantee but got the exposure of double branding. A customer's eye would see me twice and typically click to Guarantee Call because our company stood out.

**What Businesses Does Google Guarantee Help?**

As of April 20, 2020, the Job Categories that are available for the Google Guarantee through the Local Ads Platform are the following:

1. Appliance Repair Service

2. Auto Service Technician

3. Carpet Cleaner

4. Electrician

5. Event Planner

6. House Cleaner

7. HVAC Pro

8. Junk Removal Provider

9. Lawn Care Provider

10. Mover

11. Pest Control technician

12. Pet Care Provider

13. Pet Groomer

14. Photographer

15. Plumber

16. Roofer

17. Tree Service Provide

18. Water Damage Service

19. Window Cleaner

20. Window Service Provider

You can have one business that services multiple categories. For instance, as a carpet cleaner, I would select the Carpet Cleaning and Water Damage Service. The requirements for each category are different, though so you will have to follow different checklists when creating your listings.

If you want to use multiple categories, you will need to contact Google Local Ads directly to add the categories to your primary. It will not allow you to do this through the dashboard like your initial set-up.

### Who can set this up?

Another great feature of the Google Guarantee is that set-up is a breeze. No monthly PPC

or Set-up Fees are required. It's so easy that I had my location set-up in five days! You simply log in to the Google Local Ads section at https://ads.google.com/local-services-ads/

and create your dashboard. As we progress through this guide, I will add more information about the set up, and the process of getting started with Google Guarantee.

# Chapter 2: The Basics

The most important thing to do before you adopt Google Ads is to explore the platform.

This means you need to know as much as you can about Google adverts, its help center, and learn to manage your Google Ads spending.

It would be good to know where your advertisements appear and learn about other Google products that can benefit your business, such as the Google Guarantee. Aren't you glad you picked up this short guide?!

**Setting Up Your Profile**

Just like everything else in the digital world, you need to set up your Google Ads profile.

From there, you can proceed to create a web page for your adverts. Make sure to set up your time zone and currency while reviewing the campaign settings. Do not forget to submit your billing information so you can pay when you start to see leads roll in.

Once you get your profile set up, you can get started with your Local Services adverts so you can advertise your trade on Google and begin receiving leads openly from potential clients. As mentioned earlier, though, Local Services adverts are available for specific service areas and categories.

To be certain that Local Services are offered in your area, verify your business admissibility on the "signup" page. Local Services are displayed above the results of Google Search when people look for the expertise you offer within your area, so you gain an abundance of exposure when you sign up.

If you are in the United States, prospective customers can tap or click on your ad which will prompt them to call you or send you a request for a message after reviewing your ad.

Once they do, you will get a notification, as well as an email, from the Local Services adverts app.

You can respond to messages, record bookings, and manage your leads at any time through the Android and iOS applications or on the online platform. When you do receive messages, it's important send a reply to them as much as you can, regardless of whether your response is a refusal or acceptance of the service requested. If you often fail to respond to calls or messages, your advert ranking will be affected. From here, you can apply for a Google Guarantee.

### Reviews and Keeping them

An important part of a successful campaign is having 5-star reviews. I will review more details about this process in later chapters. As small business owners in the current over-opinionated society, we know how hard it can be to keep everyone happy.

Here are my tips for getting good reviews, keeping good reviews on your profile, and how to deal with bad reviews when you inevitably get them. You will get a review link for your google Guarantee Profile that you can share with past customers so they can leave you a testimonial.

Make sure to never review yourself, not only is it very unethical and bad karma for business, it is also illegal and can get you banned from all Google Platforms. I would personally recommend only emailing customers a review request to your Guarantee Profile after speaking with them on the phone so you can confirm that they were happy with their services.

The most important thing for you to do is to **maintain three stars or higher to stay on this platform**. Of course, nowadays, you must keep yourself higher than that to stay in business!

**Secret Tip On How To Get First Place All The Time** So, I am, by no means, claiming to have figured out any algorithms. But I have figured out a few things that have always kept my ads in the first place for carpet cleaning in the Charlotte Metro and Greater Metro Area.

First, I **keep 5-star reviews**. Customers can be harsh and protecting your business against folks who are on emotional roller coasters, should be key. I only ask for a few reviews a month from customers who I call and ask if they would complete a review. I want to be confident these are the customers who really:

1. Raved about my service while we were there,

2. Gave me the confidence that they were fans of my business, and
3. Gave me the idea that they want to spread the word.

Calling customers to check-in and ask for a review allows you to create a great Google Guarantee profile. Also, the call and personable after-service follow-up had these Customers raving about my business to their friends and family, which lead to lots of referrals. The free referrals you gain from this process diminishes the costs of any leads you pay for on the platform.

Next, this is a kicker. You are going to think I am crazy after I say this but I believe that my ad always shows up as #1 in the Guarantee result spots because I **set my budget for the maximum budget**, which is over $12,000! I also set my per lead cost at the highest available in the area I am serving the ads. That's right max it all out. Read on too see why.

Why would I do that? I only run two vans in this one market I am referring too, so, yes, that seems excessive. What I have figured out is that, by setting the maximum budget, which would scare everyone else, I am automatically placed in first on top of all other providers. Why is this?

Well, Google is in the business of making money, and if I am willing to spend the most, they want to make sure my ad gets the most exposure so I can get the most leads and spend as much of my budget as possible. So, they place me at the top hoping I will take the leads that come in and in turn spend large sums on money.

By moving to the top budget in my area, I automatically get the top spot. This combined with my 5-star reviews makes for an awesome conversion rate. I can assure you I am not too reckless and have great reasons to share with you that are fail-safes in my plan. The main reason I am able to set my budget so high is that **there is not enough demand**.

At the end of the day, the most I might spend in a month is $1,200 versus $12,000. A BIG

difference. I wish more people were searching and calling, and I would happily spend

more with google, and just add more trucks to my routes. Unfortunately, the budget is 80

to 90% higher than the actual demand in my field.

This gives you the top spot for spending the same as your competition. I have been in business long enough for myself that I have always **had an advertising account with an advertising card that is only used for advertising purposes**. I keep just enough in that account to cover the expected budget costs.

So, when Google runs my card at $500, if it happened outside the budgeted amount set in the account, it would automatically decline and pause my adverts creating a failsafe. I have always found that having an advertising card has been helpful since you tend to be a little more liberal with sharing the credit card number in advertising situations.

**Insurance**

Part of the Google Guarantee is having Google verifying your insurance. This typically just means your General Liability Insurance or Business Insurance. Some companies, such as movers, who are electronically required to keep their insurance on file with state and local governments, may be asked to furnish proof of Automobile and/or Cargo Insurance.

Providing this information to Google is part of the process.

# Chapter 3: About Advanced Verification

For some business categories, advertisers will be required to complete the Advanced Verification to prevent fraudulent businesses from advertising on Google using false identities.

This verification process unites a study of your Google Ads account with publicly existing data, and filmed interviews directed by Google. Checking includes investigations into business listing validity and proof of misleading or fraudulent business practices.

### Licensing

Depending on your business and the state you are located in, you may be required to show proof of license to the Google Local Ads Team. Some trades, such as locksmiths and plumbers, require licenses that are required to operate in that state. You will need to provide the Google Local Ads Team proof of your active license.

Some areas do not require licensing locally but do require it for the state. If this is the case you will still need to provide proof of licensure. This process is managed by Google. Once Google contacts you about the information, you must provide complete, honest, and accurate data.

Also, you must join a video meeting which will be recorded. After your company has been validated, you might be requested to go through a re-verification procedure annually. You will likely have to verify your business again when there are major changes, such as moving locations or change your website.

### Licensing Checks

Subject to your country, Google confirms that businesses possess applicable provincial, state, and country-level licenses representing businesses and owners or managers. The certificates Google has substantiated for each company are shown on their supplier profile.

Google may do audits to safeguard observance of the Advanced Verification processes. To stay in good repute, be certain to fully accommodate all audits. You can contact Google at any time towards identifying any error, inaccuracy, or other issues regarding the verification of your business.

If your request is denied, you will receive a notification through your email address which will give you an opportunity to present an appeal. You may, however, only make one petition for appeal. Hence, it is suggested that you review the policies from top to bottom beforehand. When handling each verification-related step, Google is bound by its Privacy Policy.

**The Checklist Required for My Carpet Cleaning Company**

1. Two reviews through my places profile;

2. Submit any people additionally insured on my Certificate of Insurance or COI; 3. Submit proof of licensing;

4. Wait for Google Verification;

5. Complete the background check, and wait for the results.

6. Create a profile to select keywords, and highlights.

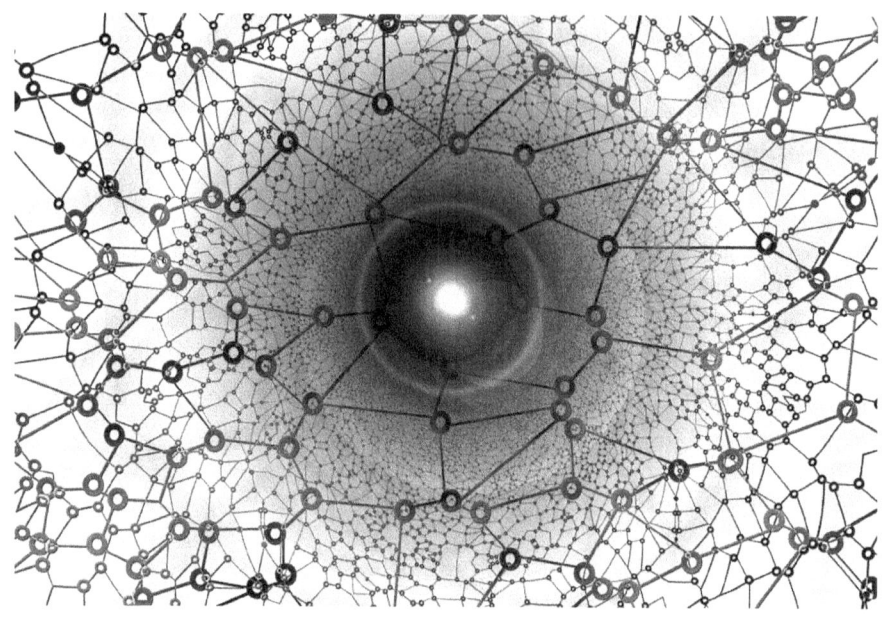

# Chapter 4: Coverage areas

Setting your coverage area is an important step. Unlike AdWords, you cannot set locations with a zip code. Instead, you will need to set the location by the town. This can be a pain if you did not serve an entire area, but just sections of an area. It cannot narrow down the area by neighborhoods.

In my case, I found the quality of leads to be so good that I increased my radius and just charged more to go further. It worked! Meanwhile, let us talk more about ads on Local Services.

### Ads Overview

Your LSA, or Local Services Ads, facilitate the attracting of clients to your trade. The highpoints of your ad are the most essential information for clients to select your business, which includes your services offered, area served, reviews, and service hours.

### How Ads Work

When you enlist for LSA, you will be asked to submit your business information that includes your service area, working hours, and offered services. This information is used to create your company profile.

Your advert will display a clip of your company profile. When users tap, or click on your ad, they will see your description. You can make changes to your information as needed.

We will discuss how you can do this in later chapters.

### What's In Your Ad?

Here is an example of how your Google Guarantee Ad may look:

50+ plumbers serving San Diego                          Sponsored

Acme Plumbing              Speedy Plumbing            Nighthawk Plumbing Se...
4.8 ★ ★ ★ ★ ★  See reviews  4.9 ★ ★ ★ ★ ★ · See reviews  4.8 ★ ★ ★ ★ ★   See reviews
● GOOGLE GUARANTEED        ● GOOGLE GUARANTEED
San Diego                  San Diego                  San Diego
(619) 555-0758             (619) 555-9927             (760) 555-8800
Open 24/7                  Open 24/7                  Open 24/7

→ More plumbers in San Diego

So, based on the image above, you can see that it contains information, as follows: 1. Business Name

2. Business Bio – This highlights the important features of your trade, such as if you offer free assessments or are locally owned.

3. Google Screened or Guarantee badge – This shows customers that they can rely on your business. We will also discuss what Google Screened is all about later in this book.

4. Location - Your company city is displayed either as your business address or the metro where you work or live. In some instances, Google may display the metropolises you service as a substitute.

5. Phone number – The number is displayed, as well as your tracking number since calls to the said number are redirected to your company phone number.

6. Photos - These pictures show prospective customers your work and business, which are also shown in your company profile when presented.

7. Reviews – These include those from Google My Business and reviews collected straight through LSA. Partner affiliate listings include reviews offered to Google via the partner website. All ads will show the average star rating for your company.

8. Work hours – These are the hours your business stays open to do business with customers.

Take note, however, that your ad format may vary once in a while. This is because Google changes the LSA format to assist you in attracting additional leads. Alternate arrangements may include extra or less info. Also, if you remain advertising via an affiliate, the information in your profile is given to Google by the partner directly.

**How to Create an Ad**

Google Guarantee does not let you create your own ad. There is no option on the platform to make an ad with the Google Guarantee. This is another reason you do not need to hire anyone to manage your Google Guarantee Campaign. All the ads are short and created by Google. You can, however, add some features that Google will highlight about your business, such as:

1. Years in Business

2. 24/7 Service

3. Free Estimates

4. Eco-Friendly

5. Military Discount

6. On Time Guarantee

7. Workmanship Guarantee

8. Tile and Grout Cleaning for Carpet cleaners only

9. Moving Labor for Movers only.

You can only select six of the options shown to you. You should consider your customer-base, and what highlights are most attractive to them. Words, such as "Free Estimates" are great eye catchers!

**COVID Options**

The offered options are:

1. Curbside Service

2. Wear Safety Gear

3. No Contact Payments

4. No Cancellation Fees

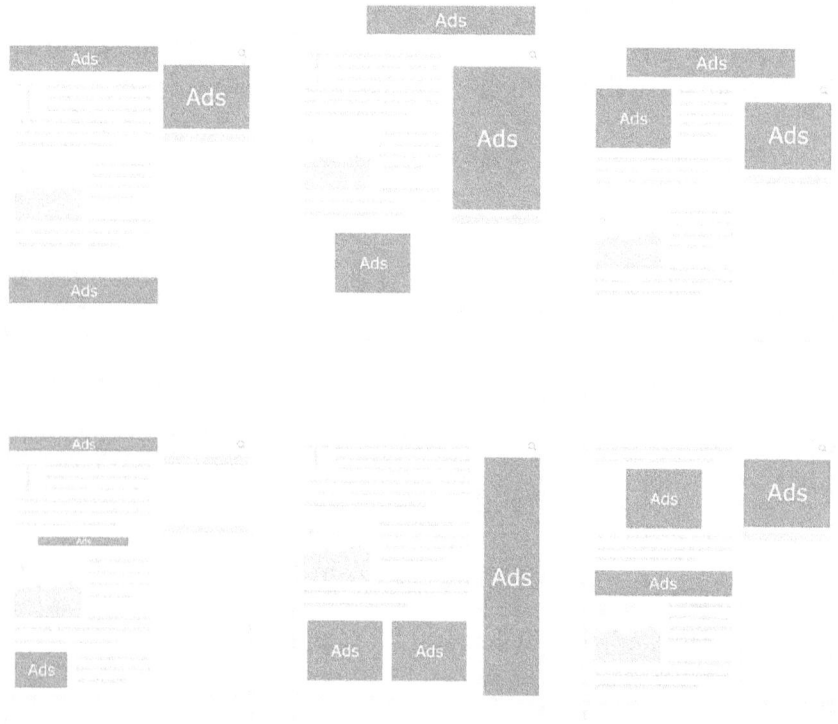

# Chapter 5: Local Service Ads

Local Service Ads provide you with the following benefits:

1. You're able to use a phone app to respond to customers at any time.

2. You can build a reputation through the Google Screened or Guarantee badge. With the Google Guaranteed badge, you are likely to be listed with a local service supplier on the platform free of charge.

3. Customers select you, and you only hear from people who are choosing you over other service providers.

4. You can speak with potential clients who are looking for facilities you provide, and these clients are likely to book your services.

5. You only pay for leads linked to your company and the facilities you offer.

6. Use simple tools that help you start and generate a tailored profile.

7. Visible at the topmost of Google!

**What Hours Should I Put for My Ad?**

The default for your hours of operations, and when your ads will show, will be for your business hours in your local profile. Selecting what days and times you want is important.

Unless you plan on answering your phone at nine o'clock in the evening, then you should not adjust the hours outside your business hours.

Again, you only pay for the leads you answer. You want to avoid customers leaving voicemails because calling customers are ready to buy. I found that they will hang up and call the next one on the list, so you really need to act fast! Also, many of these customers are looking for service within the next one to three days. So, again, do not be afraid to charge a premium.

## Scheduling Your Ad

The steps to scheduling your ad are, as follows:

1. Sign into Local Services

2. Click the menu at the top

3. Click on Profile and Budget

4. Click on the blue text next to "Ad schedule." The blue text will be whatever schedule type is currently set and as listed in the next step. The default schedule type is "Always on"

5. In the "Ad scheduling" dialog, choose the type of schedule for when you want your ad to display:

a. Always on - Your ad will run 24 hours a day, 7 days a week.

b. Only during my business hours - Your ad will run during the business hours specified in the "Business Hours" field at the bottom of the Profile and Budget page.

c. Custom Hours - Choose the days of the week and the hours of the day to show your ad.

## What about Messaging Options?

Messaging is an option you can turn on or off. I would highly recommend leaving it on.

It's worth noting that conversions are not as solid on message leads, which is why google only charges half of the cost of a phone lead for messages that may not follow through.

# Chapter 6: Managing Leads

Now that you understand the platform, and how to set up your account, the next step is watching the leads roll in. As potential customers message, and call you, you will receive alerts from the app and from your email. When you receive a call from a potential buyer, you'll want to answer as soon as possible so that they don't move on and call someone else. With messages, you have the option to reply to the customer, call them, or decline their message. The decline feature is helpful for the "tire-kickers" who aren't serious about hiring you.

### Lead Credit and How It Is Charged

Leads are charged as they come in for your business based on your monthly budget. This is the main reason that it scares people to set a $12,000 budget, because Google will continue to charge you for leads you receive until you meet that budget. For this reason, I highly recommend getting a credit card that is solely for advertising with the limit set to your actual budget. Once your credit card hits its maximum value it will be declined, and Google will temporarily pause your account. This way you won't be charged for any more leads. This allows you to be on top for having the highest budget, and only have to spend your real budget. The cost for the lead varies for different businesses and often considers the type of lead. For instance, as we mentioned in previous chapters, messages cost less than phone calls because people are less likely to be serious.

### Valid Leads

There is a big difference on Google Local Ads between valid, and invalid leads. A valid lead is a lead that you receive through that platform that have some kind of action attached to them. Examples of valid leads include:

• Texts, Emails, or Phone Calls from a Customer

- Voicemail from a Customer

- Returning a Text or Phone Call from a Voicemail

- Booking Requests Made Through the Platform

**Examples of Invalid Leads**

An invalid lead is a lead is not going to contribute to an increase in your business. There are four basic types of invalid leads:

- Spam

- Solicitation

- You Don't Offer the Service

- You Don't Serve the Location

When you receive an invalid lead on Google Local Ads, you can dispute the charge for the lead as long as it fits one of the criteria above. This is one of the other reasons I love the platform so much. Google recognizes the possibility of people who aren't serious, or who might be wasting your time, and gives you clear guidelines to refute it. You will be charged for all of the leads you receive on the platform, but you have the right to refute the charge if you believe it is not valid. If Google confirms that it's not a valid lead, you will be credited for it.

As you probably know from past experiences with other ad services, there will still be

"tire-kickers" and when those come you don't want to have to pay when you know they aren't serious. Google also makes a strong effort to recognize these types of responses before you see them, and automatically credits your account. If the message or call for some reason doesn't meet the requirements to be "invalid", you can still refute it and plead your case to Google.

It's important to note that there are some "invalid" leads that don't result in a customer conversion that Google will still charge you for. For instance, if someone calls you about the service you offer and you have a conversation, you will still be charged. You also won't be credited if the customer cancelled the service, or never responded to your message.

## Types of Charged Leads That Are Eligible for a Credit

There are several situations where you will be given a credit for charged leads. The first situation is when you go over budget, and you are charged for more leads than your budget allows. You will be given a credit, so you stay below your budget. You will never be charged for more money than you set your monthly budget.

In addition, anything that is considered an invalid lead and falls into the category of spam, solicitation, or the request being out of your field, or location, is eligible for a credit. This includes messages received from bots, or messages that do not show clear intention to hire you, as well as when the job the customer is looking for is not something you provide.

You can also dispute a lead to receive a credit if you were charged for the same customer twice in fifteen days, or the customer did not leave you any contact information to get back to them.

## How to Track Leads

The Google Local Ads give you the ability to track your leads, and the money that you're spending. You can view your billing information right on the platform so you can see how much you've paid each month, and how many leads resulted in customer conversions. You also have the ability to mark leads as "booked", this gives you the opportunity to create your schedule right on Google so you can track your business, and it also gives you the chance to send a professional-looking confirmation email to the customers who booked through Google. The platform can provide you with reports analyzing your use of the service so you can get a good idea of your return on investment.

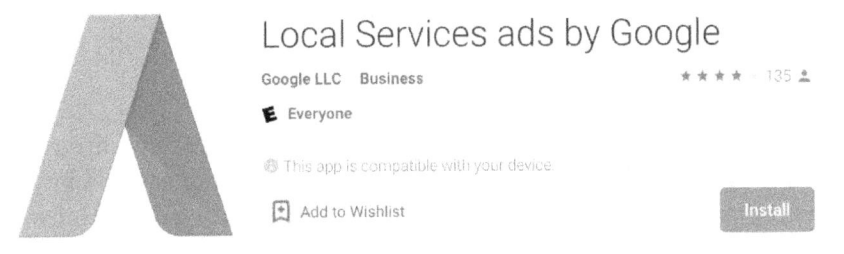

## Chapter 7: Lead Disputes and Using the App

Google continues to lead the world in its user-friendly interface. While the company is well known for being user-friendly for consumers, most people don't know that it is extremely user-friendly for businesses as well. Google makes it easy to dispute leads that you think are invalid, and also regularly checks your account to make sure you aren't paying for leads that result from spam messages. In addition, Local Services Ads has its own app that helps you to see your leads and get notifications when new people view your business.

### How to Dispute Leads

As we mentioned in the previous chapter, there are several situations where you might have a lead that is considered invalid. When this situation arises, you will want to dispute the lead with Google so you can receive a credit for it on your account.

To review, a lead might be considered invalid if it meets one of the following categories:

• Spam

• Solicitation

• Requesting a Service That You Don't Offer

• Requesting Your Services in an Area You Don't Work In

There might be other issues with leads that arise through your Local Service Ad that you may want to dispute, and Google gives you the option to do that.

Disputing leads is a very simple process that ensures you aren't paying for leads that won't bring your company business and have a zero percent chance of customer conversion. The first step to dispute a lead is to click on the menu option on the lead you believe is invalid, and then select dispute. As long as the lead fits into one of the four categories mentioned above, Google will respond within a week and let you know the lead charge will be credited to your account. If you are receiving a credit for the lead, it will show up on your billing account in the next month.

It's important to note two things about the lead dispute process.

1. Google regularly reviews your leads and will automatically credit leads that it considers to be invalid, so you may receive credits for leads you did not manually dispute.

2. The original lead charge will always be on your bill from Google for your records as well as theirs. The credit will show up within the following calendar month, but there still needs to be a record that you were charged at one point for the lead.

### Local Services Ad App

The Google App for Local Services Ads is extremely helpful in managing your Google Ads, as well as the leads that come in. Most people aren't able to be at their computers all day so it can be beneficial to get alerts on your phone when new leads pop up. This is beneficial because it allows you to immediately respond even if you are away from your desk or computer which means the customer is less likely to try to message someone else, and it also provides you with an easy interface to manage and dispute your leads on the go.

I found that this can be incredibly helpful with disputing leads because it allows me to click the dispute button right then and there when the lead comes in. If I get an invalid lead at 8 am when

I may be away from my desk, I can easily hit dispute button and not have to worry about it after that. If I don't use the app, and I have to wait until the next time I'm at my computer I might forget to dispute it and I will pay for a lead that doesn't benefit me.

The Local Services Ad App has a great interface that allows you to view your ads, leads, and account right from your phone. This is an excellent option for people who are always on the go because it allows you to manage your online business presence with little to no effort.

# Chapter 8: Costs and Payment

Before you jump aboard the Local Services Ads express, you should know the basic costs for the service before you sign up. The reason this section is so late in the book, despite being the first thing most people think about, is that I thought it was important for you to see all the amazing benefits that Google can provide to your business before you see the cost.

Don't let this section scare you away though. Once you see the average costs for leads on Google and compare that to your current advertising services or the cost to employ an advertising specialist, you will see that Google can do more for you in the long run for less money.

### How Much Will the Service Cost?

As we've discussed before, Google will only charge you for the legitimate leads so it's important to keep in mind that you won't be charged for spam messages or people who reach out to you from California for a service you offer in Maine.

The base cost to use the Google Local Services Ads is $50.00 per month, plus the cost of the valid leads that you receive based on your monthly budget and the amount of people who reach out.

The cost per lead varies by industry, and location, but the average cost that you can use to calculate an estimate is $25 per lead. This cost also varies based on the way that the customer reached out to you. Since messages are less likely to result in a hire, they typically cost less than a phone call which is more likely to guarantee a customer conversion.

The most important thing for you to consider when you are setting your budget and allocating your advertising costs is the risk vs reward of spending the money on leads. As I mentioned before, it can be beneficial to use your credit card limit as your "maximum spending" and set your google limit to the highest possible threshold. Regardless of whether you use Googles maximum limit, or the limit on a credit card, you need to consider what you really want to spend on leads, and how it will affect your business.

Consider the following scenarios:

- You set your limit for your lead budget at $100. You receive four valid leads with that money, but you only get one customer conversion which gives you a $120

profit. At the end of the day, you made a $20 profit which makes it hard to justify the cost of the advertising.

- You set your limit for your lead budget at $500. You receive 20 leads, and 5

conversions, each with a $120 profit. You make a $100 profit and gain several positive reviews which provides a boost to your business.

In the two situations listed above, there were multiple factors that impacted the success of the company's advertising. Now, I'm not saying that you should be spending $10,000 a month for advertising, but you should also consider how much you need to spend for your campaign to be successful.

### How You're Charged

Businesses are charged through the billing account they set up upon starting their Local Service Ads. This will require you to submit a valid payment method that will be charged when you make an automatic payment. Google utilizes automatic payments because it allows them to charge you in a consistent manor and helps businesses track their expenses. With automatic payments, you will either be charged on your monthly payment date, or when you reach your payment threshold.

Your payment threshold is set based on your monthly maximum allowance. When you create your account, you will set up a weekly spending limit that will determine the maximum amount of money you are willing to spend on leads. Google will then multiply that number by four to get your monthly maximum. There may be times when your expenses exceed your weekly limit, but they will never go past your monthly maximum.

## Chapter 9: Ready to Receive Leads through Local Services Ads?

Now that you've read through the last eight chapters of my book, you should be ready to sign up with Google and start letting the leads pour in so you can grow your business.

Once you sign up with Google Local Service Ads, you should know how to use the system and how to reach out to support when you need help. It's important to know that Google is very flexible for its consumers on all platforms – including businesses. Local Services Ads are made to help you succeed, so if you're having an issue on the platform it pays to reach out so you can gain a solution to your problem.

### Contact Local Services Support

As with many large companies that serve the public, Google's customer support team is incredible. As a consumer on Google you may already know that they have an abundance of options available for people who need help with a Google app. In addition to the immense support for consumers, Google Local Services Ads also offer excellent support for businesses who are using their platform. There are multiple ways to reach out to the support team for Local Services Ads:

• You can reach out to Google Support, specifically for Local Services Ads, at 1-833-272-1444 from 6 am – 5 pm Pacific Time on any weekday. This will allow you to speak to someone about the issues you're having and will help you find an immediate solution.

• You can view the Local Services Ads help center which provides many articles on common issues that people experience on the platform. This is an excellent choice when it's midnight and you're having a minor issue with your ad. You can browse problems that people have had and read about similar situations to your own.

## Free Local Services Listings

Another great feature that Google offers for businesses is Google My Business. This platform lets you create free Local Services Listings so that when people search for businesses near them, your business comes up on Google Maps.

Having an account for Google My Business also allows you to add crucial information to the listing that comes up on Google Maps when someone searches for the services you offer. The information you can add includes:

• Name of the Owner

• Hours for your Business

• Phone Number

• Website

• Links to Social Media Pages

Using this feature is an excellent way to get attention for your business without having to pay for leads, or other services. The downside to this service is that you are only able to get customers who search your location and choose your page so it's important to make sure you have as much information as possible. There's nothing customers hate more than having to spend five minutes just to find your phone number.

# Chapter 10: Google Screened

One of the final steps that you will have to take once you set up your Google Local Services Ads account is going through the final screening process so you can become a Google Screened business. As we discussed in earlier chapters when we discussed Google Guarantee, this is beneficial because it reassures potential customers that your business has been verified and is legitimate. When you go through the google screening process you, and your employees have to receive background and licensure checks so Google can be sure you are a legitimate business.

While this is a ton of work for the business owner, once it's complete you get a new badge for your Google listing which shows potential customers that you are have been Google Screened. This gives customers a huge reassurance when they are looking for new services because they know you're someone they can trust.

### How It Works

The process to become Google Screened involves both background checks, and licensure checks for you and your staff. The first step is a background check for the business itself to make sure the company is legitimate, and then a background check for the business-owner, or manager. Your employees may have to pass either a licensure check, a background check, or both depending on the type of industry.

These background checks are crucial for many industries because people get peace of mind knowing the employees that are working closely with them, and possibly entering their homes have been vetted thoroughly.

### Who Google Screened Covers

The Google Screened process is still a fairly new service that started in August of 2019.

For this reason, there are a lot of industries that it does not cover at the moment. Of course, as Google continues to grow, and businesses continue to support the Local Services Ad industry the industries under Google Screened can grow as well.

Right now, the following types of businesses are eligible for Google Screened:

• Law Firms

• Real Estate Companies

• Financial Planning Companies

**Reports**

Another wonderful feature that Google provides to its Local Services Ad users is reports on the status of their ads. Google breaks down a lot of the information that you are getting from your ad campaign and analyses it to help you get an understanding of how you're doing.

Local Services Ad reports help with two main sets of data. They track the amount of leads you are getting from your ads on Google, and if you are using the features that let you manage your leads, Google tracks how many of those leads turn into customer conversions when they book appointments with you. This feature is especially easy to use if you also use the online booking feature that Google provides. If you don't use the booking feature, you can also mark leads as booked when you manage them.

In addition to those benefits, Google allows you to specify what data you want to see and filter it out. You can track:

• The leads you received within a certain time frame, and how much you spent within that time frame for the leads.

• A list of the specific leads you received which can be filtered based on specific criteria, such as which leads were valid and which ones you disputed.

- If you use the booking feature, it will break down which specific leads resulted in bookings and what your booking rate (or customer conversion rate) is for a certain time period.

I've found the reports to be extremely helpful because it saves you time when you need specific data about how your ad is doing. If you're like me, and you've been around the block in the world of advertising then you know how much of a pain it can be to do this analysis yourself. They give you the data you need, when you need it with little to no effort on your end.

**Using the Dashboard**

The dashboard for Google Local Services Ads is extremely helpful for tracking leads. It breaks down your leads for you into five categories and allows you to make changes if necessary – such as disputing a lead or marking it as booked.

The first tab that you'll see is your new leads, these are the leads that have just come in that you haven't seen yet. The next tab is active leads which are the leads you have received and have either called back or responded to their message. Once you book a service for a customer, their lead moves into the booked tab, and once the service is done then it moves to the completed tab. Then, there's a final tab that you'll see is for inactive leads.

The dashboard is an excellent function that allows you see all of your leads in the same place, and also allows you see what needs to be done. You can see all of your incoming leads, as well as leads you might have replied to but were waiting on a response. From this page, you can also dispute any leads that you feel meet the criteria, or are invalid for another reason, and you can mark the leads as booked and completed so that your reports have the most up to date information.

⊘ GOOGLE GUARANTEED

# Make it easy for customers to choose you

Stand out with an upgraded Business Profile and the Google Guaranteed badge. Just **$50/month** for eligible businesses.

**Upgrade profile**

By continuing you agree to the Onboarding terms. They include the use of binding arbitration to resolve disputes rather than jury trials or class actions.

Google

Sheryl's Cleaning

Sheryl's Cleaning
⊘ GOOGLE GUARANTEED
5.0 ★★★★★ (40)
Open · Closes 7 PM

# Chapter 11: Local Services Onboarding Terms

Like all other platforms, Google has a set of terms that you have to sign in order to use their services. Most people never read these terms, because they're long and complicated, so they just sign the form and click "done". I think that it's important to read through the terms for the Local Services Ads Onboarding, so I've explained the main points of the text below. At the very least, review the basic summaries of each section below so that you're aware of the terms which you are agreeing with when you sign the form.

### Information You Submit

The first section of the Local Services Onboarding Terms is pretty simple. This section basically states that when you create your account you will be asked for personal information, which is covered under Google's privacy policies.

This section is not extremely important, because with any advertising platform it can be assumed that you're going to need to provide personal information so your customers can learn about your business. This information can also include your businesses location and phone number which would be publicized on the page for your ad.

### Minimum Provider Requirements

Google's minimum provider requirements are the basic verification requirements that are asked of businesses when they create their account. These requirements can be found online, but they basically include information about the age of your employees, and your adherence to other legal business requirements. Google wants to ensure that you meet these requirements while you are using their Local Services Ads and can deny your access to the platform if you don't meet the requirements at any time.

## Indemnification and Limitation of Liability

This section protects Google from all legal situations by requiring that you defend Google, and anything related to Google in the event that there is a third-party lawsuit against you or your team.

## Employment

This is a pretty straightforward requirement, but it basically just states that you cannot employee a Google employee, or anyone related to Google to participate in your business.

## Notice of Changes

Google reserves the right to make any changes to the contract at any time, if the change is significant you will be notified. If there is a small change that does not affect the agreement, the change will be made without a notification.

## Dispute Resolution Agreement

This is the section that you want to review thoroughly because it includes the premises for a dispute with Google. I have written down the basic points included in the terms, but it is also a good idea to read it for yourself to gain a full understanding.

- You and Google will come to an agreement on any issue that arises regarding disputes and claims.

- You waive your right to a trial and jury, as well as the ability to participate in a class action class suit against Google.

- You must provide Google's legal department with written notification of a dispute if you would like to file one.

- The AAA rules will apply to any claims less than $75,000. If the claim is less than $25,000, the AAA will decide whether there will be a hearing.

• If you wait 60 days to begin the arbitration with AAA after filing your dispute, or ff it's less than 60 days after submitting notice but your claim is less than $75,000

Google will pay the filing fees.

• You have 30 days to opt out of a dispute.

**Miscellaneous**

The final section of the terms concludes the contract, and states that all claims will be governed by California law as that is where Google Headquarters is located, and the courts will be located in Santa Clara County.

# Chapter 12: FAQs

The final section of this book will be dedicated to frequently asked questions that people have in regard to Google Local Services Ads, and Google Guarantee.

### What is Google Local Services Ads?

Google Local Services Ads are a feature that businesses can sign up for that create ads for your business when people search for certain keywords. For example, if you have a plumbing business in Phoenix, and I live in Phoenix and search "Plumbers near me" your business can come up with an ad explain your hours and description.

### How Can I Get 5 Star Reviews?

On a very basic level, the answer to this question is to do good work. On a deeper level, there are things you can do to ensure you get good feedback such as calling a customer after a service to follow up, and only requesting reviews from customers who you know will rave about you online.

### What is Google Guarantee?

Google Guaranteed is a badge that you can earn when you go through a verification process with Google. This badge helps you get more business because when people see

that you have been verified with Google, they get extra peace of mind, and are more likely to hire you compared to someone who hasn't been verified.

### How much does Google Local Services Cost?

The cost for Google Local Services Ads varies based on the area you work in, but it is typically a $50 per month base charge, plus $25 dollars per valid lead.

## What's a Valid Lead?

A valid lead is any lead where the person shows interest in your business. The customer does not have to book with you or hire your service to be considered valid, but they do have to meet certain criteria. If the lead is clearly spam, or solicitation, or the person is asking for a service you don't provide or asking you to provide a service outside of your area, the lead is considered invalid and you can get a refund.

## Is Google Local Services Ads Beneficial for Small Businesses?

The short answer is yes! Google Local Services Ads may seem scary at first to small businesses who don't have a lot of money to allocate for advertising, but the leads that you receive from Google compared to other platforms are extremely high quality. The platform is an excellent choice for small businesses looking to find new customers or expand to a larger area.

## What Kind of Data Can I Get from Google Local Ads?

Google provides a lot of great information regarding your ads, and the leads that you receive from them on the platform. The reports and dashboards section that Google uses is perfect for managing your leads because it gives you one location to see your new, active, inactive, booked, and completed leads and allows you to track your spending for specific time periods.

## Conclusion

Use this guide to serve as a reference in setting up your Local Ads Google Guarantee Ads.

If you are a small Service Business just getting into the Guarantee program, no worries, your leads should be able to cash flow themselves from day one. The first day I turned on Google Guarantee I scheduled 2 jobs worth $420 and only spent $63 to get them. With results like this you can quickly and economically add Customers and revenue to any service business that Local Ads allows in the Guarantee program.

Best of luck! Feel free to email directly at jeremy@jeremygoding.com if you have any questions or feedback.

*-- Jeremy Goding*

www.ingramcontent.com/pod-product-compliance
Lightning Source LLC
Chambersburg PA
CBHW070855220526
45466CB00005B/2007